DIPHTHERIA COOKBOOK GUIDE 2023

"Nourishing Meals for Recovery and Wellness"

By

PROF. FRANK ANTHONY ROBERTS

Copyright © [2023] by [Prof. Frank Anthony Roberts]

TABLE OF CONTENTS

Introduction

Hello and welcome to "The Diphtheria Cookbook Guide: Nourishing Your Recovery."

Proper nutrition is a cornerstone of healing in the area of health and well-being. This idea is especially important while fighting diphtheria, a bacterial infection produced by Corynebacterium diphtheriae. Diphtheria predominantly affects the respiratory system, offering a serious risk to people who are infected. The essence of this cooking guide is recognizing the importance of eating in the rehabilitation process.

In the following pages, we shall delve into the complexities of diphtheria, from its origins and manifestations to its probable consequences. Understanding this ailment is essential for understanding the function that a deliberate, balanced diet plays in the healing process.

As we progress through the chapters of this guide, we will discover the complex relationship between diet and diphtheria recovery. Each segment is meticulously constructed to demonstrate the importance of a well-planned diet in not only reducing symptoms but also strengthening the body's natural defenses.

Our goal is to provide a complete resource for diphtheria patients, caregivers, and healthcare professionals who want to improve their healing path with good nutrition.

From soft and soothing dishes to immune-boosting recipes, this guide aims to empower readers with knowledge and culinary solutions that contribute to a swifter and more wholesome recovery.

Let's embark on this voyage together, dedicated to enriching lives and fostering recovery through the power of nourishing foods.

1.1 A description of diphtheria

This section gives readers important details regarding the bacterial infection known as diphtheria, which is brought on by Corynebacterium diphtheriae. It discusses topics like the nature of the illness, its symptoms, transmission methods, risk factors, and probable side effects related to diphtheria. Readers must comprehend the disease in order to appreciate the value of a healthy diet in controlling and recovering from it.

1.2 Diet's Importance in Diphtheria Recovery

Proper diet is critical in the rehabilitation process for people suffering with diphtheria. A well-balanced and nutritious diet is necessary for a variety of reasons. To begin, proper diet strengthens the immune system, assisting the body in fighting off the diphtheria infection. Vitamins, minerals, and proteins are essential for the immune response and the repair of injured tissues.

Second, keeping sufficient nutrition can aid in the management of diphtheria symptoms and consequences. To relieve the discomfort produced by a sore throat and swallowing issues, soft and readily swallowable foods are frequently recommended. This dietary change guarantees that the patient gets the nutrients they need without worsening their disease.

Moreover, the right diet can provide the energy needed for the body to heal and recover. Diphtheria can cause weakness and fatigue, making it crucial to consume nutrient-rich foods that boost energy levels and aid in the healing process.

In summary, a well-considered diet is not only instrumental in managing diphtheria symptoms but also in supporting the body's recovery and minimizing the risk of severe complications.

CHAPTER ONE

2. Diphtheria Patients' Nutritional Foundations

This section offers the framework for understanding the critical function of diet in helping diphtheria patients recover. Nutrition is critical in providing the body with the basic building blocks needed for healing, energy maintenance, and immune system strengthening. It intends to assist readers in making educated food choices that will have a major influence on their recovery.

2.1 Nutrients Required for Healing

This section digs into the essential nutrients required for healing during and after a diphtheria infection. It discusses the significance of macronutrients like proteins, carbs, and fats, as well as micronutrients like vitamins and minerals. Understanding how these nutrients contribute to tissue regeneration, immunological function, and general recovery enables people to customize their diets to provide a balanced and healing-focused nutritional intake.

2.2 Tailoring the Diet to Individual Needs

Recognizing that each individual's nutritional needs may vary, this sub-section emphasizes the importance of personalized dietary approaches for diphtheria patients. Factors such as age, underlying health conditions, severity of the infection, and personal preferences are taken into account when tailoring a diet plan. This ensures that the nutritional requirements of the individual are met, optimizing the healing process and aiding in a faster and more effective recovery.

CHAPTER TWO

2. Creating a Diphtheria-Friendly Diet

This section is dedicated to assisting diphtheria patients, carers, and healthcare professionals in developing a meal plan that meets the nutritional requirements and limitations associated with diphtheria. A well-planned meal arrangement is vital for guaranteeing nutritional intake while taking into account the obstacles offered by symptoms such as difficulty swallowing and general weakness. This section provides information on creating a balanced, nutritional diet plan to help in the healing process.

2.1 Planning Balanced Meals

This sub-section focuses on the importance of incorporating a variety of nutrients in each meal to create a well-rounded, balanced diet for diphtheria patients. It provides insights into how to include adequate amounts of protein, carbohydrates, healthy fats, vitamins, and minerals in meals. By emphasizing portion sizes and food combinations, this sub-section aids in developing nutritious meal plans that cater to the specific dietary needs of individuals affected by diphtheria.

2.2 Ingredients and Recipes

We explore into the practical aspects of meal planning in this part by providing a variety of diphtheria-friendly recipes and emphasizing necessary products. The recipes have been carefully selected to ensure that they meet the nutritional needs and dietary concerns required for diphtheria recovery. Furthermore, we give information on readily available items that may be utilized to produce these nutritional meals, making meal planning and preparation more easy and effective.

CHAPTER THREE

3. Soft and Nourishing Dishes for Diphtheria Patients This section is dedicated to presenting soft-textured and easily swallowable dishes appropriate for individuals recovering from diphtheria. These dishes are meticulously designed to provide the necessary nutrition without causing discomfort during swallowing or exacerbating the symptoms of sore throat commonly experienced by diphtheria patients. By offering a range of gentle and nourishing options, this section aids in ensuring a nutritious and soothing dietary approach throughout the recovery process.

3.1 Smoothies and Shakes

This sub-section explores the versatility and nutritional benefits of smoothies and shakes, making them ideal choices for diphtheria patients. Smoothies and shakes are not only soft and easy to consume, but they can also be packed with essential nutrients, vitamins, and minerals. The sub-section provides various recipes tailored to suit the dietary requirements of individuals recovering from diphtheria, focusing on flavors and ingredients that are soothing to the throat and gentle on the digestive system.

3.2 Soups and stews

Soups and stews are warming, soothing foods that are easily digested and may be tailored to satisfy the nutritional requirements of diphtheria patients. This section delves into a variety of soup and stew recipes that focus both flavor and nutrition. These recipes may be made with soft ingredients, making them easier to swallow while also supplying important nutrients to aid in recuperation. The sub-section additionally emphasizes the application of particular ingredients to enhance flavor and nutritional value while keeping the textures suitable for those in recovery.

3.2.1 Comforting Chicken and Vegetable Soup

Ingredients:

- 1 cup boneless, skinless chicken breast, cooked and shredded
- 2 carrots, peeled and chopped
- 2 celery stalks, chopped
- 1 small onion, finely chopped
- 2 cloves garlic, minced
- 4 cups low-sodium chicken broth

- 1 cup water
- 1 cup cooked rice or small pasta (optional)
- Salt and pepper to taste
- Fresh parsley for garnish

Instructions:

1. In a pot, sauté the onions and garlic in a little olive oil until translucent.
2. Add the carrots, celery, chicken broth, and water. Bring to a boil and then reduce to a simmer.
3. Add the shredded chicken and let the soup simmer until the vegetables are tender.
4. If using, add the cooked rice or pasta and let it simmer for a few more minutes.
5. Season with salt and pepper to taste.

6. Serve in a bowl, garnished with fresh parsley.

3.2.2 Hearty Lentil and Vegetable Stew

Ingredients:

- 1 cup dried lentils, rinsed and drained
- 1 onion, chopped
- 2 carrots, peeled and chopped
- 2 celery stalks, chopped
- 3 cloves garlic, minced
- 4 cups vegetable broth
- 1 can (14 oz) diced tomatoes, undrained
- 1 teaspoon dried thyme
- Salt and pepper to taste
- Fresh parsley for garnish

Instructions:

1. In a large pot, sauté the onions and garlic until softened.
2. Add the lentils, carrots, celery, vegetable broth, diced tomatoes, and thyme. Bring to a boil, then reduce to a simmer.
3. Let the stew simmer until the lentils and vegetables are tender, stirring occasionally.
4. Season with salt and pepper to taste.
5. Serve in a bowl, garnished with fresh parsley.

3.2.3 Soothing Potato Leek Soup

Ingredients:

- 3 leeks, white and light green parts only, chopped
- 3 large potatoes, peeled and diced
- 4 cups low-sodium vegetable broth
- 1 tablespoon olive oil
- 1/2 cup low-fat milk or non-dairy milk
- Salt and pepper to taste
- Fresh chives for garnish

Instructions:

1. In a large pot, heat olive oil over medium heat. Add the leeks and sauté until softened.

2. Add the diced potatoes and vegetable broth. Bring to a boil, then reduce the heat and simmer until potatoes are tender.
3. Use an immersion blender to puree the soup until smooth.
4. Stir in the milk and season with salt and pepper.
5. Reheat if needed and garnish with fresh chives before serving.

3.2.4 Gentle Vegetable and Rice Stew

Ingredients:

- 1 cup cooked rice
- 1 cup carrots, peeled and diced
- 1 cup zucchini, diced
- 1 cup spinach leaves, chopped

- 4 cups low-sodium vegetable broth
- 1 teaspoon olive oil
- 1/2 teaspoon dried oregano
- Salt and pepper to taste
-

Instructions:

1. In a pot, heat olive oil over medium heat. Add carrots and sauté for a few minutes.
2. Add zucchini and continue to sauté until slightly tender.
3. Pour in the vegetable broth, add cooked rice, and bring to a simmer.
4. Stir in dried oregano and season with salt and pepper.
5. Add the chopped spinach and simmer until the vegetables are cooked to your liking.

6. Adjust seasoning as needed and serve warm.

CHAPTER FOUR

4.1 Packed with Proteins:

Diphtheria and Meat Alternatives are Protein-Rich.

This section emphasizes the necessity of getting enough protein into diphtheria patients' diets, covering both lean animal sources and plant-based alternatives. Proteins are required throughout the healing phase for tissue regeneration, immunological function, and general strength. This section guarantees that persons recuperating from diphtheria may satisfy their dietary demands adequately by providing a varied selection of protein-rich options.

4.1.1 Lean Protein Options

In this section, we look at numerous lean protein sources that are good for those recuperating from diphtheria. Lean proteins are critical for muscle rehabilitation and development because they provide needed amino acids for mending. Skinless poultry, fish, low-fat dairy, and other lean protein sources are highlighted in the subsection, highlighting their significance in a well-rounded recovery diet and their capacity to help in restoring strength throughout the healing process.

4.1.2 Plant-Based Protein Options

Recognizing the importance of offering diverse dietary options, this sub-section focuses on plant-based protein alternatives suitable for diphtheria patients. Plant-based proteins not only provide essential amino acids but also offer additional benefits such as fiber and various vitamins and minerals. The sub-section discusses plant-based protein sources like legumes, tofu, tempeh, nuts, and seeds, enabling individuals to choose protein-rich options that align with their dietary preferences and restrictions.

4.2 Lean Protein Options

4.2.1 Chicken Breast Grilled

Skinless, boneless chicken breast is an excellent source of lean protein. Grilling or baking it gives for a healthier cooking option that minimizes extra fat while preserving the natural tastes. Chicken breast is high in protein, low in fat, and readily digested, making it an excellent choice for diphtheria patients looking to increase their protein intake.

4.2.2 Baked Fish

Fish, such as cod, haddock, or tilapia, provides high-quality protein with minimal saturated fats. Baking the fish preserves its nutritional value and delicate texture, making it easy to consume. Incorporating baked fish into the diet can be a flavorful way to enhance protein intake and support the recovery process.

4.3 Plant-Based Protein Alternatives

5.3.1 Legumes

Lentils are an excellent plant-based protein source. They are flexible and simple to make; they may be added to soups, stews, salads, and even cooked into lentil patties. Lentils are high in protein, fiber, and many vitamins and minerals, making them an excellent plant-based protein option for diphtheria patients.

4.3.2 Chickpeas (Garbanzo Beans)

Chickpeas are a staple in plant-based diets and offer a substantial protein boost. They can be used in salads, curries, or blended to make hummus. Chickpeas are not only protein-rich but also provide essential nutrients like iron, folate, and dietary fiber, making them an excellent addition to a recovery-oriented diet.

CHAPTER FIVE

5. Recipes that are Easy on the Throat: **Soft and Comforting**

This section focuses on offering relaxing and readily digestible meal alternatives for those recuperating from diphtheria. The idea is to provide mild recipes that reduce pain during swallowing while yet providing adequate nutrients. This section seeks to offer a wonderful and soothing culinary experience during the recuperation period by using purees, mashes, puddings, and custards.

5.1 Purees and Mashes

In this sub-section, we explore recipes that are soft in texture and easily pureed or mashed, making them gentle on the throat.

Pureed vegetables, fruits, and well-cooked grains are at the heart of these recipes. The sub-section provides a variety of options that can be customized to suit individual tastes and dietary needs, ensuring a comforting and nourishing culinary experience.

6.2 Puddings and Custards

This sub-section offers comforting dessert-like recipes that are soft, creamy, and easily consumed, making them ideal for individuals with sore throats. Puddings and custards provide a pleasant taste while being gentle on the throat. The recipes featured here cater to those looking for a touch of sweetness in their recovery diet, ensuring that even during challenging times, there's a bit of indulgence to be found in the world of soft and soothing foods.

CHAPTER SIX

6.   Nutritional   Immune Enhancement

This section stresses the vital role diet plays in boosting and strengthening the immune system, particularly throughout the diphtheria recovery phase. Its goal is to give advice on how to incorporate immune-boosting foods into the diet, with an emphasis on increasing the body's natural defensive systems through a nutrient-rich approach. This section seeks to empower individuals to maximize their recovery and general well-being by emphasizing certain nutrients and antioxidants that stimulate a robust immune response.

6.1 Foods to Strengthen the Immune System

In this sub-section, we delve into a variety of foods that are known to bolster the immune system. These include fruits, vegetables, nuts, seeds, and other wholesome options packed with vitamins, minerals, and other immune-boosting nutrients. Understanding the benefits of these foods and how they contribute to a stronger immune response equips individuals with the knowledge needed to make informed dietary choices during the recovery period and beyond.

6.2 Antioxidant-Rich Options

Antioxidants play a crucial role in immune support by neutralizing harmful free radicals in the body. This sub-section focuses on foods rich in antioxidants, such as berries, citrus fruits, leafy greens, and nuts. Antioxidant-rich options are essential for mitigating oxidative stress and inflammation, promoting a healthy immune system. By incorporating these foods into the diet, individuals can contribute to their overall recovery and long-term wellness.

6.3 Foods that Help the Immune System

6.3.1 Citrus Fruits

Citrus fruits such as oranges, grapefruits, lemons, and limes are high in vitamin C, a potent antioxidant that helps the immune system. Vitamin C promotes the development of white blood cells, which are necessary for combating infections. Including citrus fruits in your diet can help you maintain a healthy immune response.

6.3.2 Spinach and Leafy Greens

Leafy greens, such as spinach, kale, and Swiss chard, are abundant in vitamins A and C, as well as antioxidants. These nutrients are vital for maintaining a healthy immune system and supporting overall well-being. Including leafy greens in the diet contributes to a nutrient-dense and immune-boosting eating pattern.

6.4 Antioxidant-Rich Options

6.4.1 Nuts and Seeds

Nuts and seeds, such as almonds, walnuts, chia seeds, and flaxseeds, are packed with antioxidants like vitamin E. Additionally, they provide essential fatty acids and minerals that contribute to overall immune health. Including a variety of nuts and seeds in the diet can be a convenient way to boost antioxidant intake.

6.4.2 Berries

Berries like blueberries, strawberries, and raspberries are rich in antioxidants, particularly flavonoids and vitamin C. These antioxidants help combat oxidative stress and inflammation, supporting the immune system's ability to function optimally. Berries can be a delightful addition to various dishes and snacks.

CHAPTER SEVEN

7. Using Medicinal Herbs and Spices

This section focuses on the beneficial incorporation of medicinal herbs and spices into the diet, which aids in the healing and general well-being of diphtheria patients. Medicinal herbs and spices have long been valued for their medicinal powers and taste enhancers. This section advocates the use of natural components that can contribute to both health and flavor by studying their use in culinary traditions.

7.1 Herbal Infusions and Teas

We explore into the world of herbal teas and infusions in this section, showcasing their possible health advantages. Herbal teas, which are frequently brewed from diverse plants, flowers, and herbs, have long been prized for their medicinal benefits. These beverages provide a gentle method to include medicinal herbs into one's everyday routine, whether for relaxation, digestion, or immune support. The section goes through how to choose and prepare herbal teas that can help with recuperation and well-being.

7.2 Spices for Health and Flavor

This section stresses the dual significance of spices, both in terms of flavor and possible medicinal effects. Spices not only improve the flavor and perfume of meals, but they also contain substances that may benefit one's health. Spices have a long history of therapeutic usage, ranging from anti-inflammatory properties to digestive help.

The section delves into several spices, their possible health benefits, and how they may be included into a diet to aid recovery and enhance the gastronomic experience.

7.3 Herbal Teas and Infusions

7.3.1 Chamomile Tea

Chamomile tea is known for its calming properties, aiding in relaxation and better sleep. It may also help soothe a sore throat. Steep dried chamomile flowers in hot water for a comforting herbal infusion.

7.3.2 Peppermint Infusion

Peppermint is often used to support digestion and alleviate discomfort. A warm infusion made from peppermint leaves can provide relief for an upset stomach or digestive issues.

7.4 Spices for Healing and Flavor

7.4.1 Turmeric

Turmeric is prized for its anti-inflammatory properties due to curcumin, its main active ingredient. It can be added to various dishes, particularly stews and soups, to enhance flavor and potentially aid in reducing inflammation.

7.4.2 Ginger

Ginger is known for its digestive benefits and potential to alleviate nausea. It can be used in both sweet and savory dishes, such as teas, soups, or as a spice in cooking, offering a zesty and healing flavor.

CHAPTER EIGHT

8.1 Tips for Safe Food Handling during Recovery

This section provides essential guidance on safe food handling practices, particularly tailored to individuals in the recovery phase from diphtheria. Maintaining proper food hygiene and taking necessary precautions against contamination are crucial during this time to ensure a smooth and risk-free recovery. By outlining key practices and measures, this section aims to promote a safe and healthy dietary experience for those on the path to healing.

8.1.1 Maintaining Food Hygiene

In this section, we emphasize the need of maintaining high standards of food hygiene while recovering. To avoid the transmission of hazardous bacteria or germs, proper food hygiene includes thorough washing of utensils, surfaces, and hands. It also entails storing and handling food at the proper temperatures to prevent bacterial development. Individuals can reduce their risk of foodborne disease and successfully assist their recovery path by following certain hygiene measures.

8.1.2   Contamination-Free   Meal Precautions

This section contains particular measures that people recuperating from diphtheria should take to ensure that their meals are free of contamination. It covers themes including avoiding cross-contamination, storing perishable foods properly, and safe food preparation practices. Taking these procedures decreases the likelihood of ingesting contaminated food, supporting a safe and sanitary dietary pattern during the recovery time.

8.2 Ensuring Food Hygiene

8.2.1 Hand Hygiene

Frequent and thorough handwashing with soap and warm water for at least 20 seconds before and after handling food is essential. This simple practice helps prevent the spread of harmful bacteria and viruses that can cause foodborne illnesses.

8.2.2 Clean Cooking Environment

Maintaining a clean cooking environment involves regularly sanitizing kitchen surfaces, cutting boards, knives, and other utensils used for food preparation. Keeping the kitchen clean reduces the risk of cross-contamination and ensures the safety of the prepared meals.

8.3 Contamination-Free Meal Precautions

8.3.1 Keep raw and cooked foods separate.

To avoid cross-contamination, keep raw meats, poultry, shellfish, and eggs apart from cooked meals and fresh produce. Separate cutting boards and utensils should be used for raw and cooked foods.Implementing these precautions significantly reduces the chances of consuming contaminated food, promoting a safe and hygienic dietary routine during the recovery period.

8.3.2 Proper Food Storage

Store perishable foods, like dairy, meats, and leftovers, in the refrigerator at 40°F (4°C) or below to slow bacterial growth. Use airtight containers to prevent odors and flavors from mingling.

9.2.3 Thoroughly Cook Foods

Ensure that all foods, especially meats, are cooked to their appropriate internal temperatures to kill harmful bacteria. Use a food thermometer to verify the correct temperature is reached during cooking.

8.4. Ensuring Food Hygiene

8.4.1 Hand Hygiene

Frequent and thorough handwashing with soap and warm water for at least 20 seconds before and after handling food is essential. This simple practice helps prevent the spread of harmful bacteria and viruses that can cause foodborne illnesses.

8.4.2 Clean Cooking Environment

Maintaining a clean cooking environment involves regularly sanitizing kitchen surfaces, cutting boards, knives, and other utensils used for food preparation. Keeping the kitchen clean reduces the risk of cross-contamination and ensures the safety of the prepared meals.

CHAPTER NINE

9. Recovery and Beyond: A Dietary Approach for Life

This final part highlights the necessity of a long-term nutritional strategy for those who have recovered from diphtheria. Recovering from an illness is only the first step; keeping a balanced and healthy diet is critical for long-term well-being. This section seeks to motivate individuals to focus their health and continue their recovery efforts by giving assistance on transitioning to a regular diet and establishing a healthy lifestyle after recovery.

9.1 Return to a Regular Diet

This section delves into the gradual shift from the specialized diet necessary for healing to a typical, well-rounded diet. It is critical to reintroduce a range of foods back into the diet while monitoring the body's reaction and modifying as necessary. Individuals can continue a broad and balanced diet that fits their nutritional demands as they advance beyond the healing period with proper transitioning.

9.2 Maintaining a Healthy Lifestyle After Rehabilitation

This section focuses on taking a holistic approach to health that extends beyond dietary factors. A healthy lifestyle includes regular physical exercise, enough relaxation, stress management, and regular medical examinations. It highlights the significance of taking a holistic approach to health, striving for long-term well-being while reducing the risk of future health problems.

Conclusion

In the journey of recovery from diphtheria, nourishment plays a pivotal role—a role that extends far beyond the boundaries of illness. This guide, "The Diphtheria Cookbook Guide: Nourishing Your Recovery," has been meticulously crafted to provide not just a collection of recipes, but a pathway towards renewal, strength, and lifelong well-being.

As you've journeyed through these pages, you've witnessed the remarkable ability of food to heal, sustain, and empower. From soothing soups to protein-packed meals, each recipe embodies the essence of recovery—a testament to the incredible power of nutrition in the face of adversity.

But this journey doesn't end here. It transitions into a new phase, one that involves embracing a regular diet while continuing the pursuit of a healthy, vibrant life. The lessons learned here, the insights gained, and the nourishing choices you make will echo into your future.

Encouragement

Dear reader, your recovery is a story of resilience, strength, and the triumph of the human spirit. You've faced the challenges head-on, and you've emerged stronger. As you move forward, remember the nourishment that fueled your recovery is the same nourishment that will sustain your journey ahead.

Embrace each meal as an opportunity to cherish your health and vitality. Choose wisely, not just for your taste buds but for your well-being. Savor the goodness that nature provides, and let it fortify you.

Life is a precious gift, and your well-being is the key to unlocking its limitless potential. Stay committed to a lifestyle that nurtures both your body and soul. Engage in physical activities that invigorate you, cultivate relationships that bring joy, and seek moments of tranquility amidst the chaos.

You are not alone on this path. You have the ability to design your own future and the strength to overcome any obstacle. Continue to nurture your body, spirit, and dreams. You have the ability to shape a future filled with health, pleasure, and contentment.

Stay fed and bright, and let your path inspire the rest of the world.

Diphtheria cookbook guide